42 BIBLE STORIES FOR LITTLE ONES

From Creation to Pentecost

Published in 2008 in the U.S. and Canada by
The Word Among Us Press
9639 Doctor Perry Road
Ijamsville, MD 21754
www.wordamongus.org

ISBN: 978-1-59325-138-3

First edition 2008
Reprinted January 2010

Publishing Director: Annette Reynolds
Editor: Nicola Bull
Art Director: Gerald Rogers
Pre-production: Krystyna Kowalska Hewitt
Production: John Laister

Printed in Singapore

Su Box and Graham Round

42 BIBLE STORIES FOR LITTLE ONES

From Creation to Pentecost

Contents

1 GOD MAKES THE WORLD 8

2 THE GARDEN OF EDEN 10

3 NOAH'S BIG BOAT 12

4 THE FLOOD AND A RAINBOW 14

5 ABRAHAM TRUSTS GOD 16

6 GOD KEEPS HIS PROMISE 18

7 JACOB THE TRICKSTER 20

8 JOSEPH'S BEAUTIFUL COAT 22

9 JOSEPH GOES TO EGYPT 24

10 THE PRINCESS AND THE BABY 26

11 "LET GOD'S PEOPLE GO!" 28

12 ESCAPE FROM EGYPT 30

13 THE WALLS FALL DOWN 32

14 A VOICE IN THE NIGHT 34

15 SAMUEL CHOOSES A KING 36

16 DAVID AND GOLIATH 38

17 GOD TAKES CARE OF ELIJAH 40

18 GOD SENDS FIRE 42

19 THE GIRL WHO HELPED 44

20 DANIEL AND THE LIONS 46

21 JONAH AND THE BIG FISH 48

22 THE BABY IN THE MANGER 50

23 ANGELS BRING GOOD NEWS 52

24 FOLLOWING A STAR 54

25 JESUS AND THE FISHERMEN 56

26 ANOTHER SPECIAL FRIEND 58

27 DOWN THROUGH THE ROOF 60

28 THE TWO HOUSES 62

29 A STORM ON THE LAKE 64

30 JESUS HELPS A LITTLE GIRL 66

31 JESUS FEEDS A CROWD 68

32 THE MAN WHO HELPED 70

33 THE GOOD SHEPHERD 72

34 "I CAN SEE!" 74

35 THE MAN WHO CLIMBED A TREE 76

36 "HERE COMES THE KING!" 78

37 A VERY SAD DAY 80

38 A VERY HAPPY DAY 82

39 THOMAS BELIEVES 84

40 A PICNIC BREAKFAST 86

41 JESUS IS TAKEN BACK TO HEAVEN 88

42 GOOD NEWS FOR EVERYONE 90

1
God makes the world

I n the very beginning, there was nothing – and it was as dark as the darkest night.

Then God began to make our world.

First God made light and called it "day." And he called the darkness "night."

God made the sky and the seas and the land on the round spinning earth. He made tall mountains and deep valleys and sandy deserts. Then

God filled the land with leafy plants and beautiful flowers and tall trees.

God made the hot sun to give light in the daytime and the silvery moon to shine at night. And he filled the night sky with twinkling stars and planets.

Then God made living things: shining fish to swim in the sea, singing birds to fly in the sky, and animals of all shapes and sizes.

God was pleased with everything he had made. It was very good. But God was not finished.

He wanted people to look after everything he had made. So God made the first man and the first woman. Their names were Adam and Eve. God loved them very much.

He wanted them to be happy and to enjoy his good new world.

2
The garden of Eden

God had given Adam and Eve a beautiful place to live in. It was called the garden of Eden, and they were very happy there.

The garden was filled with delicious fruits and vegetables. Adam and Eve could eat anything they wanted, except from one tree.

This special tree grew in the middle of the garden.

"It is called the tree of knowing good and bad," said God. "You mustn't eat any of its fruit. If you do, everything will be spoiled."

One day God's enemy came into the garden. He didn't like the beautiful garden, and he wanted to spoil everything God had made and planned.

He crept up to Eve and hissed in her ear.

"God was lying when he told you about that tree. You won't die if you eat its fruit. You will be wise, just like God!"

Eve looked at the tree. The fruit looked so delicious. She took a big bite. Then she gave some to Adam.

Suddenly they knew they had made a mistake. The garden didn't look the same anymore. They didn't feel the same anymore. Everything was spoiled. They had disobeyed God, and they hid from him.

But God knew what had happened. He was very sad. He had made Adam and Eve to love him, and he loved them.

"You cannot stay here," said God. "You did not do what I said. You did what you wanted, and now everything is spoiled."

So Adam and Eve left the beautiful garden of Eden forever.

3
Noah's big boat

Many years passed, and the world became a very unhappy place. People were mean and unkind. They fought and argued all the time. They had all forgotten about God.

When God saw how bad everyone was, it made him very, very sad. This was not what he wanted. He began to wish that he had never made the world.

But there was one good man who still loved God. His name was Noah. Noah tried to do what God wanted, and God was very pleased with him.

One day God spoke to Noah. "I wish I had never made the world," he said. "I am going to start again. I am going to flood the earth with

water and wash it clean."

God told Noah to build a very big boat. He told him exactly how it should be made. So Noah cut down trees and hammered in nails. Then he covered the boat with thick, sticky tar to keep the water out.

Everyone thought Noah was crazy! They laughed at him for building a boat so far from the sea. And they would not listen when Noah told them what God was going to do.

At last Noah's big boat was ready. God told Noah to fill the boat with animals. He had to take two of every creature with him and enough food for a long, long time. So Noah did what God had told him.

"Take your family with you, too," said God. "I will keep all of you safe when the big flood comes."

4
The flood and a rainbow

It was going to rain. Noah and his family and all the animals were safely inside the big boat, so God shut the door.

Drip! Drip! It began to rain.

Pitter-patter! The rain grew harder.

Splish! Splash! Splosh! The rain poured down, filling the streams and rivers. The rivers burst their banks, and the seas flooded the land.

Soon the boat was afloat! It rained and it rained for days and days. At last everything on earth was covered by the flood. There was nothing to see but water everywhere.

But the boat was still afloat. And Noah and his family and all the animals were safe and dry inside.

Many days passed. Then God sent a wind, and the waters began to go down.

Noah found a raven inside the boat and set it free. But the bird could not find any dry land.

Noah waited a few days. He found a dove inside the boat and set it free. But the bird came back. There was still no dry land.

Noah waited a little longer. Then he sent the dove out again. This time it came back with an olive leaf in its beak. It had found dry land!

A few days, later God told Noah to leave the boat. The animals slithered and crawled and hopped and leaped onto the dry land. They were happy to be free again.

"Thank you, God, for keeping us safe!" said Noah.

"I will never destroy the earth with a flood again," said God. "This is a sign of my promise."

Noah looked up – and saw a brightly colored rainbow glowing in the sky.

5
Abraham trusts God

Abraham and his wife, Sarah, lived happily together. But they longed to have children.

One day God spoke to Abraham. "I want you to leave your home," he said. "You are to go on a long journey. I will show you the way. I am going to give you a new land to live in."

Abraham was surprised, but he trusted God.

Then God gave Abraham a bigger surprise. "I am going to give you a family," said God. "One day everyone will hear about you, and your family will become a great nation."

"A family means children," thought Abraham. Excitedly, he went to tell Sarah what God had told him.

"We must pack up our things and go where God leads us," Abraham said to Sarah. So Abraham and Sarah, and their servants, and their cows and camels, and their sheep and goats, set off on their journey.

They walked and they walked. Every day they found grass for the animals to eat. Each night they stopped and put up tents to sleep in.

They did not know where they were going. But Abraham knew that God would show them the way because he had promised to be with them wherever they went.

It was a long, long journey. But at last they reached the land of Canaan. Abraham could see a river, green grass, and tall trees. This would be a good place to live.

"This is the land that I will give to you and your children," said God.

"Thank you," said Abraham. And he put up his tent for the last time.

6

God keeps his promise

Abraham and Sarah were getting old. They longed for a son but still did not have any children. Sometimes they were sad, but they trusted God to help them.

One day Abraham was talking to God.

"I will look after you," God promised. "And I will give you more than you can imagine!"

"But what I really want is a baby boy," Abraham told him. "And

now we're too old to have children."

"I promise that you will have a son of your very own," said God. "Look up at the sky!"

Abraham looked up. The night sky was full of twinkling stars.

"Can you count the stars?" asked God.

Abraham shook his head.

"Your family will be as many as the number of stars!" said God.

Abraham still had no children. But once again he trusted God.

Some time later, Sarah had a lovely baby boy. She called him Isaac. Sarah and Abraham were very happy.

Abraham knew that Isaac was a very special baby. God had kept his promise.

7

Jacob the trickster

Many years later, when little Isaac had grown up, he married a beautiful girl named Rebekah. Their sons, Esau and Jacob, were twins, but the two boys were very different.

Esau was born first. When he grew up, he loved to be outdoors,

running about and hunting. His father, Isaac, loved Esau best.

Jacob liked to stay at home with his mother, Rebekah. He was her favorite son.

When their father was an old man, the time came for him to give his eldest son, Esau, a special blessing. This meant that Esau would be the head of the family after his father had died. One day all the good things God had promised to his grandfather Abraham would be his.

"Before I bless you, go and get some meat for a special meal," said Isaac. So Esau went out hunting. Rebekah saw the chance for Jacob, the younger son, to get the blessing instead of Esau.

"Quick!" she said. "I will make your father's favorite meal, and you can pretend to be Esau."

"It won't work. Esau's arms are hairy, not like mine," said Jacob.

"Don't worry," said Rebekah. "You can wear Esau's clothes. Then wrap some animal skins around your arms so that your skin feels hairy like Esau's. Your father will never know, and you will get his blessing!"

Jacob did what Rebekah said. He took the food and went in to his father's tent.

"Is that really you, Esau?" said Isaac. He was very old, and he could hardly see.

"Yes, Father," lied Jacob. Isaac reached out and touched Jacob's arms, which were covered in animal skins. They felt exactly like Esau's hairy arms.

And so Isaac gave his special blessing to Jacob instead of to Esau.

8

Joseph's beautiful coat

Old Jacob had a big family. He had twelve sons and one daughter. Out of all of them he loved his young son Joseph best of all.

One day Jacob gave Joseph a special present. It was a beautiful, brightly colored coat. None of his brothers had anything like it.

Joseph was pleased. He wore his beautiful coat as often as he could. He liked to show it off. He would say, "Look at me. Look at my special coat."

Joseph's big brothers were jealous. They saw how much their father loved Joseph. They did not like Joseph's beautiful coat. They did not like Joseph, either. He was bossy and boastful.

One day Joseph's big brothers were out working, taking care of their father's sheep.

"Go and see how your brothers are," said his father. So Joseph set off, wearing his beautiful coat.

His brothers saw him coming.

"Here comes Joseph!" groaned one of them.

"I've had enough of him!" said another.

"Let's kill him!" said a third. "No one will know. We could say he's been eaten by a wild animal!"

"No. Don't kill him," said Reuben, the eldest brother. "Throw him down this empty well instead."

So Joseph's brothers grabbed him and tore off his beautiful coat.

"No more showing off now," said one brother.

Then they threw Joseph down into the well.

But even at the bottom of the empty well, God was looking after him. God had plans for Joseph.

9
Joseph goes to Egypt

Poor Joseph was at the bottom of an empty well. He begged to be let out, but his brothers would not listen. They had taken his beautiful coat, thrown him in the well, and left him.

"That will teach him," said one of them. Then the brothers sat down to eat.

"Look!" said Judah. In the distance, they could see a long line of people and camels. They were traders, on their way to Egypt with spices and other things to sell.

"I've got an idea!" said Judah. "Let's sell Joseph to those traders. Then we'll be rid of him!"

The brothers were very pleased. They thought it was an excellent idea.

When the traders came near, the brothers pulled Joseph out of the well. Before long they had sold him for twenty silver coins.

Now Joseph belonged to the traders. They took him to faraway Egypt to be a slave!

Then the brothers tore his beautiful coat, dipped it in animal blood, and went back home.

"Look what we've found!" they said to their father, showing him the coat. "It looks like Joseph's coat!"

Jacob looked. He saw the coat. He saw the blood. "A wild animal must have killed Joseph," he cried. He was very unhappy. He was sure that Joseph, his favorite son, was dead.

But Joseph was alive. He was safe and well in Egypt. God took care of Joseph. God was with him.

10

The princess and the baby

Many years had passed since Joseph's time. God's people, the Israelites, had been living in the land of Egypt for a long time. It was not their own country, and they wanted to go home. But they were slaves. They could not escape.

One day the Egyptian king had a horrible idea.

"There are too many of these people in Egypt," he said. "We will kill all their baby boys."

God's people were very frightened. Their babies were in danger. One woman, named Jochabed, kept her baby boy a secret. At first he slept a lot and it was easy.

But the little baby grew and grew. He chuckled and gurgled. He wriggled and kicked. He made more and more noise. Soon someone would find the secret baby!

"I cannot hide him any longer!" said the baby's mother. So she wove a basket with a lid and made it waterproof. Then she put the baby inside the basket and hid it in the reeds by the River Nile.

The baby's sister watched and waited to see what would happen. She made sure her brother was safe.

After a while, an Egyptian princess came down to the river and saw the basket. What could be inside? Could she hear a baby crying? The princess opened the basket and found the baby.

"Don't cry," she said. "I will look after you."

"I know someone who can help you!" said the baby's sister. She ran to get her mother.

"Look after this baby," said the princess. She did not know that she was talking to the baby's mother. "When he is old enough, he can come to live with me at the palace. His name is Moses."

11
"Let God's people go!"

Moses grew up like a prince and lived in the Egyptian palace. But he did not belong there. He was one of God's people, an Israelite.

The other Israelites were slaves in Egypt. They had to work hard all day, making bricks in the hot sun. They wished they could leave Egypt and go to their own land.

One day God said to Moses, "My people are unhappy. I want you to be their leader. I want you to tell the king of Egypt to let them go!"

Moses did not want to be a leader. He was frightened of the king. But he did as God told him.

"God wants you to let his people go!" said Moses bravely. But the king said, "No!"

Then the king said, "Make the Israelites work harder."

"Do what God says or bad things will happen," Moses warned the king. But the king said, "No!"

Then things began to go wrong for the king.

God told Moses to hit the River Nile with his shepherd's stick. The water turned red, like blood.

"Let God's people go!" said Moses. But the king said, "No!"

"Listen to God, or there will be trouble!" said Moses. But the king said, "No!"

Suddenly there were frogs in the food, frogs in the houses, frogs in the beds! Everywhere there were frogs.

"Let God's people go, or there will be more trouble!" said Moses. But the king said, "No!"

Soon the land of Egypt was covered in biting insects, then swarms of flies. All the cows died, and the people broke out in spots. Hail fell like stones from the sky, and the crops were eaten by locusts.

Then an inky darkness covered Egypt.

"All right," said the king at last. "You can go!"

12

Escape from Egypt

The king of Egypt had told God's people they could leave his country. Then he changed his mind. He would not let the Israelites go home.

God was angry. He spoke to Moses, the leader of the Israelites. "Tell my people to get ready to leave Egypt," he said. "Something terrible will happen tonight, so that the king will beg you to go."

The Israelites got ready. They packed their bags and put on their coats. They ate a special meal. God told them to paint a special sign on their houses so that they would be safe.

Then, in the middle of the night, God came to Egypt. All the Israelites were safe in their houses, but in every Egyptian house something terrible happened. Some of the animals and some of the people died, including the king's son.

The king of Egypt sent for Moses. "Take God's people and go!" he shouted.

The Israelites left as quickly as they could. They took all their belongings and animals with them. Everyone was happy and excited. They were on their way home!

But they had not gone far when the king of Egypt changed his mind again. "We need our slaves. Who will work for us now?" he said. "Get the chariots ready. We'll bring them back!"

The Israelites were by the Red Sea when they heard the gallop of horses and the clatter of chariots. The Egyptians were chasing them. They were trapped!

"Don't be afraid," said Moses. "God is with us."

Moses stretched out his hand across the water. Suddenly a strong wind blew and made a path through the water. All the Israelites and their animals walked across on dry land.

When everyone was on the other side, the water rolled back. The Egyptians could not cross over, and God's people were safe.

13

The walls fall down

It took many years for the Israelites to get back to their own country. They had many adventures, but God was always with them.

Now the Israelites were near the city of Jericho, and the king of Jericho was scared. The Israelites were coming! Everyone had heard of how the God of the Israelites had rescued them from Egypt. Their God was strong and mighty. And their God had promised to give the city of Jericho to them.

Jericho had big, high walls made of stone. It had huge, wooden

gates to let people in and out. But now the gates were shut tight, and all the people were inside.

The Israelites had a new leader. His name was Joshua. He was brave and he loved God.

"I will help you capture Jericho," God told Joshua. "This is what you must do."

Joshua listened to God's plan. Then, for six days, seven priests marched once around the city walls. They blew their trumpets and carried the special box that held God's laws. The Israelite army marched behind them.

On the seventh day, the seven priests and the army marched six times around the city walls. But when they marched around the seventh time on the seventh day, Joshua cried, "Shout! For God has given us the city of Jericho!"

The priests blew their trumpets and the people shouted! And the big strong walls started to crack and crumble. The stones wobbled and shook until they finally crashed to the ground.

The Israelites rushed into the city. God had let them win, just as he had promised.

14

A voice in the night

Samuel was special. His mother, Hannah, knew that even before he was born. And she had promised that her son would serve God all his life.

So when Samuel was old enough, Hannah took him to Shiloh, where people came to worship God. Samuel stayed there with old Eli, the priest, who looked after him and taught him all about God.

One night Samuel was lying in bed. It was dark in the room

except for a small lamp burning dimly. Eli was asleep in another room. Everything was quiet and still, and Samuel was nearly asleep.

Suddenly he heard a voice say, "Samuel!"

"It's Eli," he thought. Samuel threw back his bed cover, got up, and ran to Eli.

"Here I am," he said. "You called me."

"No, I didn't!" said Eli. "Go back to sleep."

So Samuel lay down again and tried to go to sleep.

"Samuel!" said the voice again.

He went back to Eli. "Here I am," he said.

"I didn't call you," said Eli. "Go back to sleep."

"Samuel!" said the voice a third time.

Samuel rushed back to Eli. What was happening?

This time Eli, who was old and wise, knew who was speaking to Samuel.

"God wants to speak to you," he said. "If you hear him again, say, 'Speak to me, Lord. I'm listening.'"

Samuel went back to bed and waited.

"Samuel! Samuel!" said the voice.

Samuel took a deep breath. "Speak to me, Lord," he said. "I'm listening."

From that day, Samuel became wise and good because he listened to God. And when he grew up, people listened to him and to what God had told him to tell everyone.

15
Samuel chooses a king

King Saul was the king of Israel, but God was not pleased with him. The next king would be good. God had already chosen him.

One day God spoke to Samuel the prophet, his special messenger. "Go to Bethlehem," said God. "I have chosen one of Jesse's sons to be the next king of Israel."

Jesse had eight sons. Seven of them were big and strong. They were tall and handsome. But their little brother David wasn't grown up yet. He was a shepherd boy.

David took good care of his father's sheep. He took them to places where there was grass to eat and fresh water to drink. Sometimes he frightened away lions or bears that came to steal lambs. Sometimes he killed them with a stone, which he threw from his sling. David trusted God to look after him.

Samuel asked to meet Jesse's sons. The first was big and strong. "He would make a good king," thought Samuel. But God said, "He's not the one I have chosen."

Then Samuel saw Jesse's second son. He was big and strong. "He would make a good king," thought Samuel. But God said, "He's not the one I have chosen."

Samuel met seven of Jesse's sons. They were all big and strong. They were all tall and handsome. But God had not chosen any of them to be king. Samuel was confused.

"Have you any more sons?" Samuel asked Jesse.

"I'll call my youngest boy, David," said Jesse. "He's looking after my sheep."

When David arrived, God said to Samuel, "He's the one! He's not as big and strong as his brothers, but he is good, and he loves me. I have chosen David to be king."

Samuel was pleased that David would be the next king. But he and David kept it a secret for many years until King Saul died.

16
David and Goliath

Some of David's brothers were soldiers in the Israelite army. Everyone in the army was frightened, very frightened. But their enemies, the Philistines, were not frightened at all. They had a giant on their side. Goliath was very, very tall. He had big strong arms and big strong legs and a very loud voice. And he carried a big sharp sword.

Every morning Goliath marched in front of the Israelites. He took a big deep breath and bellowed, "Who will come and fight me?"

But nobody wanted to fight Goliath. He was much too fierce and much too big.

One day David, the shepherd boy, came to the Israelite camp to see his brothers. When he heard about Goliath, he was angry. "We shouldn't be frightened," he said. "We've got God on our side!"

So David went to the king and said, "I will fight Goliath! I have kept my sheep safe from bears and lions," said David. "I don't need a sword or armor. All I need is my shepherd's sling and five small stones."

David walked bravely toward Goliath.

This made Goliath angry. "They dare to send a boy to fight me!" he roared.

"You have a big sharp sword," shouted David. "But I

have the living God on my side!"

Goliath stepped forward. Quickly David put a little stone in his sling. He whirled it around his head and took aim… And the little stone flew through the air and hit Goliath – right in the middle of his forehead.

CRASH! The giant crashed to the ground. Now the Philistines were frightened and ran away. David had won!

17
God takes care of Elijah

Elijah was one of God's prophets – he told people what God asked him to say. He was one of God's special friends.

But bad King Ahab did not like God. He did not want to listen to what Elijah had to say. He got angry with the prophet, so angry that Elijah had to run away.

At that time it had not rained in Israel for many, many days. The rivers were dry and the fields were dry. There was nothing to eat and nothing to drink.

"Don't worry," said God to Elijah. "I will look after you."

And God told Elijah where to find a little stream. Now he had plenty to drink. He heard the flutter of wings, and some birds hopped up to him.

They had food in their beaks. Each day, the birds brought him bread and meat. Now Elijah had plenty to eat.

But one day the little stream dried up.

"Don't worry," said God to Elijah. "I will look after you."

And God told Elijah where to find a woman who would help him.

"Please give me something to eat," he asked her.

"I've only got enough for me and my little boy," said the woman.

"God will look after you," said Elijah. "Please share your food

with me."

So the woman took Elijah home. She made some bread with her flour and oil. Then she and her little boy and Elijah ate the bread. She had no food left.

But then the woman looked again. There was plenty of flour! The oil jar was full! She could make a lot more bread!

"God will look after you," said Elijah. "You will always have something to eat!"

18
God sends fire

Bad King Ahab's wife was even more wicked than he was. Her name was Jezebel, and she worshipped a god called Baal.

"We don't care about the living God!" said the king and queen. Instead they bowed down to statues of Baal.

God was very angry with Ahab and Jezebel. He sent Elijah to them with a message.

Ahab knew that Elijah was a good man sent by God.

"What do you want?" he asked crossly.

"A competition," said Elijah, "between your god and mine!"

So Ahab and Jezebel and all the people who worshipped Baal went with Elijah to the top of a high mountain.

"Let's make a sacrifice to God on an altar," said Elijah. The priests

of Baal built an altar and piled it high with wood. Then Elijah built an altar, too.

"Now let's ask our gods to send down fire. The god who can do this must be the living God," said Elijah.

"O Baal, answer us. Send down fire!" shouted the priests of Baal. Nobody answered.

"O Baal, send down fire!" they begged. Nothing happened.

The priests danced around the altar. "Please send down fire!" they cried. Still no fire came. This went on for hour after hour, and there wasn't even a puff of smoke.

Elijah teased them. "Perhaps Baal is asleep?" he said.

Then Elijah poured water over the wood on his own altar.

Elijah didn't shout and dance. He simply prayed, "Please show everyone here that you are the living God."

Suddenly the wood on his altar burst into flames. The fire burned up the water. The fire burned up the sacrifice. There was nothing left. Elijah's God had sent fire!

Everyone fell to the ground.

"Elijah's God is the living God," they said.

19

The girl who helped

Naaman was a brave and important soldier in the Syrian army. But Naaman was sad. Little white spots had appeared on his body. Soon nobody wanted to go near him, in case they caught the spots, too. Everyone was worried.

Naaman's wife had a little Israelite servant girl who wanted to help. She was far from home, but she trusted in the God of Israel.

"Would my master go to Israel?" asked the girl. "The prophet Elisha could make him better."

Naaman's wife told her husband what the little girl had said. And so Naaman went to Israel to find God's servant, Elisha. He knocked on the door. But Elisha did not answer.

Instead, Elisha's servant came with a message: "Elisha says you must wash seven times in the River Jordan."

Naaman was angry. Naaman stamped his feet. "Huh!" said Naaman. "I thought that Elisha would at least come to touch me. I

thought he would speak to me himself. I might as well have stayed at home and washed in one of our rivers!"

"Excuse me, sir," said one of his servants. "If Elisha had asked you to do something difficult, you would have done it. Why don't you do what he says? It's easy."

So Naaman went down to the river. It was deep, so he could duck right under the water. Naaman washed in the water once. He washed in the water twice. He washed in the water three, four, five, and six times. Water splashed everywhere. But Naaman's skin was still covered in spots.

Then Naaman washed for the seventh time in the River Jordan. This time the spots vanished!

Naaman wasn't angry anymore. "Now I know," he said, "that there is only one true God in all the world. And he is the God of Israel!"

20
Daniel and the lions

Daniel lived in the land of Babylon, far from his home in Israel. He was a good man who loved and worshipped God.

Daniel worked hard and did not tell lies. King Darius was pleased with Daniel. One day the king said to Daniel, "I am going to put you in charge of my kingdom."

But there were some bad men in Babylon who were jealous of Daniel. The bad men grumbled. The bad men complained. The bad men did not want Daniel to be in charge. They wanted to get Daniel into trouble, but he never did anything wrong. Then the bad men had an idea.

"You are such a great king!" they said to King Darius. "Why don't you make a new law? For the next thirty days, no one must worship

anyone but you. If they do, they will be thrown into a den of lions!"

This sounded like a good idea, so King Darius made the law.

Daniel was happy to work for the king, but he would not worship him. Instead, he worshipped God, just as he had always done. This was just what the bad men had wanted!

The bad men told King Darius what Daniel was doing. The king was sad. He liked Daniel, but even he could not change the law.

So Daniel was thrown into the pit where the lions lived. They had sharp teeth and hungry tummies. That night the king could not sleep.

In the morning, the king rushed to the lions' den. "Daniel?" he shouted.

"I am here, my King!" Daniel answered. "God sent an angel to close the lions' mouths!"

King Darius was so pleased. He made a new law. "From now on," he said, "everyone must worship Daniel's God!"

21
Jonah and the big fish

Jonah was one of God's prophets – he gave people messages from God.

"The people in Nineveh are very, very bad," said God one day. "I want you to go to that city and tell them to stop what they are doing, or they will be punished."

Jonah did not want to go to Nineveh. Instead, he ran away. He got on a ship, paid his money, lay down in his bunk, and fell fast asleep.

The ship set sail. Soon a strong wind began to blow, and the waves grew higher. The ship went up, up, up and down, down, down on the rough sea.

The sailors prayed to their gods, but the storm got worse. They were very frightened. "We're going to drown!" they cried.

Then they saw that Jonah was asleep.

"Wake up!" they shouted. "We're going to die!"

Jonah knew that the storm was his fault. He had disobeyed God. "Throw me into the sea!" he said. "Then the storm will stop raging."

So the sailors threw Jonah into the sea. At once, the storm stopped raging. The ship was safe.

Jonah was sinking down into the water when God sent along a huge fish. It opened its big mouth and swallowed Jonah in one big GULP!

It was very dark inside the fish. It was very smelly, too. Jonah was stuck there for three days!

"I'm sorry!" Jonah prayed to God at last. "I shouldn't have run away." Then the big fish swam near the shore and spat Jonah up onto the sand.

"Go to Nineveh," said God again. And this time Jonah went.

Jonah told the people of Nineveh that God loved them, but he didn't like them doing bad things. The king and all the people of Nineveh listened to God's message. They said they were very sorry and stopped being nasty. And God did not punish them.

22

The baby in the manger

Mary lived in the little town of Nazareth. She was going to marry a carpenter named Joseph.

One day, when Mary was at home, she had a surprise visitor. The angel Gabriel came to her with a message from God! At first Mary was frightened. She had never seen an angel before. Why had an angel come to see her?

"Don't be afraid," said Gabriel. "God is very pleased with you. You are going to have a very special baby. He is special because he is God's only Son. You will call him Jesus. He will bring peace to the whole world!"

Mary was amazed! She did not really understand. She took a deep breath.

"I want to do whatever God wants," she said.

Some months later, Mary and Joseph had to go to Bethlehem, where Joseph's family came from. The Roman rulers wanted everyone to go to their hometown so they could be counted. It was a long way, and Mary was tired. Soon her baby would be born.

Bethlehem was busy. Lots of other people had traveled there, too. Mary and Joseph tried to find somewhere to stay, but everywhere was full.

At last Joseph knocked on the door of an inn.

"Do you have somewhere we could stay?" he asked the innkeeper.

The innkeeper shook his head. But then he thought of his stable. It was dirty and smelly, but it was dry and warm.

Mary was happy to stay in the stable. She knew her baby would be born soon. Joseph made her a warm place to rest, and that night Mary's very special baby was born.

Mary gently wrapped baby Jesus in strips of cloth and laid him down to sleep in the soft straw in a manger.

23

Angels bring good news

On the night that Jesus was born, some shepherds sat huddled together for warmth on a hillside near Bethlehem. They took turns watching their sheep, keeping them safe through the long, dark night.

Suddenly a bright, bright light shone in the darkness. What was this? The shepherds hid their eyes. They were frightened.

"Don't be afraid!" a voice called out.

That made the shepherds even more frightened! They looked up into the sky and saw a bright, shining angel.

"God has sent me with some wonderful news for the whole world!" said the angel. "A very special baby has been born in Bethlehem. He is the one God has promised, who will put things right in the world. Go to

Bethlehem and see him for yourselves! You will find the baby asleep in a manger."

Suddenly the whole sky burst into light. There were angels everywhere. The angels danced and the angels sang:

"Glory to God in heaven.

And peace to all people on earth."

When the angels had gone, the excited shepherds left their sheep and ran all the way to Bethlehem. They hurried through the quiet streets and found the stable. Carefully they pushed open the door.

In the stable, they saw Mary, Joseph, and the baby Jesus asleep in the manger. It was just as the angel had said.

"Thank you, God!" said the shepherds. "We have seen your very special baby!"

Soon it was time for them to go back to their sheep. And all the way, the shepherds sang praises to God for what they had seen and heard.

24
Following a star

When Jesus was born, God put a special star in the sky. Far, far away, in another country, there lived some wise men. They saw the new star, and they knew it meant something special.

"This star is a sign," said one.

"A new king has been born!" said another.

"Let's go and find him," they decided.

So the wise men set off on a long, long journey, following the

star. Where would it lead them? At last they reached the big city of Jerusalem.

"A king must live in a palace," said the wise men. So they went to the palace. But only King Herod lived there.

"We are looking for the new king," they said. "Is he here?"

King Herod was surprised. Then he was worried. Then he was angry! He did not like the sound of a new king.

"Go to Bethlehem," he said. "When you find the new king, come back and tell me where he is. Then I can go to worship him." But King Herod was not telling the truth. He had secret plans, plans that were wicked.

So the wise men left Jerusalem and followed the star. It led them to a little house in Bethlehem. They went inside and found Mary and little Jesus.

The wise men knelt down and gave him presents of gold, frankincense, and myrrh – special gifts that were just right for a king.

"Thank you, God, for this new king," said the wise men. "Thank you for sending the star to show the way!"

That night God sent an angel to warn the wise men. "King Herod's plans for the child are bad. Don't tell him where he lives," the angel said.

So the wise men went back home by a different way.

25

Jesus and the fishermen

Now Jesus was grown up, and he had special work to do. He wanted everyone to hear the good news about God. Jesus began his work by Lake Galilee. It was a busy place, and lots of people worked there.

One day Jesus was watching the fishermen. Some of them were mending their nets. Others were selling their fish from big baskets.

Jesus saw a little fishing boat, not far from the shore. Two of his friends were in the boat. They were throwing their nets into the water, hoping to catch some fish.

"Peter!" Jesus called. "Andrew!"

When the two brothers saw Jesus, they waved.

"Come with me!" called Jesus. "Let me teach you all about God! Leave your fishing and come and be my special friends. Then you can

help other people find out about God."

At once, Peter and Andrew dropped their nets. They jumped out of their boat, swam to the shore, and went with Jesus.

Jesus walked around the lake. He saw two more brothers, James and John, sitting in their fishing boat with their father, Zebedee.

They were getting their nets ready for their next fishing trip.

"Come with me!" called Jesus.

At once, James and John jumped out of their boat, swam to the shore, and went with Jesus.

The four fishermen left everything behind – their work, their home, and their families. They wanted to follow Jesus and learn about God.

26
Another special friend

Matthew lived in the town of Capernaum, where he collected money called taxes. He worked for the Romans, the people in charge of the country where Jesus lived. People didn't like the Romans. And they didn't like tax collectors – they were always cheating people.

One day, Matthew was sitting at his table, collecting money. Jesus walked up to him. But Jesus had not come to pay his taxes.

"Come with me," said Jesus. "Leave your work and follow me."

At once, Matthew stood up. He left his work, and went with Jesus.

"Come to my house," Matthew said. "Let's have a meal together. You bring your friends, and I'll bring my friends."

So Jesus had dinner at Matthew's house. There were lots of other tax collectors there, as well as Matthew's other friends. Most of them were people nobody liked. Jesus talked to everyone. He wanted to be friends with everyone.

There were people called Pharisees who thought they were very good. They saw Jesus at Matthew's house. The Pharisees didn't like Matthew or his friends. They said the things they did were bad.

The Pharisees went to Jesus' friends. "These are bad people," they said. "Why are you friends with bad people? Why are you friends with Jesus?"

Jesus heard what they were saying. "Anyone who wants to can be my friend," Jesus said.

Matthew became one of twelve very special friends of Jesus. They were called "disciples," and they went everywhere with Jesus.

27

Down through the roof

News had spread that Jesus could make people well again – he was a very special healer. So, many sick people came to ask Jesus to help them and make them better.

There was a man who could not walk. He couldn't even move. He just lay on a mat all day. He longed to be made well. But how could he get to see Jesus?

This man had four kind friends.

One day the four friends heard that Jesus was visiting their town. So they thought of a way to take their friend to see Jesus. They were sure that Jesus could help him.

They carried the man on a mat through the town to the house where Jesus was. But everyone wanted to see Jesus! There were so many people in the house that there was no room for anyone else.

Then the four friends had an idea. Outside the house were some steps going up to the roof. Very carefully, they carried the man up the steps. Very carefully, they started to make a hole in the roof!

Everyone inside the house looked up. They were surprised!

The four friends made the hole bigger. And bigger. Then they let the man on the mat down into the room!

Jesus looked at the four men. He knew how much they wanted to help their friend. Then he looked at the man lying on the mat. The man looked at Jesus.

"God forgives all the bad things you have done," said Jesus. Then he said, "Stand up! Pick up your mat and go home."

The man sat up. The man stood up. The man bent down and picked up his mat. The man walked!

"Praise God!" he said, looking at Jesus.

Everyone was amazed.

"Praise God!" they shouted.

And the man walked home.

28

The two houses

Jesus was a good teacher. Crowds of people would come to hear him talk. They especially enjoyed listening to his stories. One day Jesus told a story about two men and the houses they built.

"One man was wise," said Jesus. "'Where shall I build my house?' he thought. 'Shall I build it near the river? Shall I build it near the sea? Shall I build it in a field? No! I will build it on solid rock!'

"So the wise man began to build his house. Building on rock was hard work. It took a long time. But when the house was finished, the wise man was very pleased.

"Soon afterward there was a terrible storm. The wind howled. The rain poured. The rivers grew higher and higher.

"The wise man's house trembled and creaked. It shivered and shook, but it did not fall down. It was built on solid rock.

"The other man was foolish. 'I don't care where I build my house,' he said. 'Anywhere will do! I'll build it on the sand.'

"So the foolish man built his house on the sand. The soft, smooth sand was easy to work with. It didn't take long to build. And when the house was finished, the foolish man was very pleased.

"When the terrible storm came, the foolish man's house trembled and creaked. It shivered and shook. It wibbled and wobbled. Then it crashed to the ground with a loud BANG!

"The foolish man's house fell down because it had been built on sand."

Jesus looked at the people who were listening to him. "If you listen to me and then you do what I say," he said, "you will be like the wise man who built his house on the rock."

29

A storm on the lake

Jesus and his friends were by Lake Galilee. It was a huge lake, almost as big as the sea.

Jesus had been busy healing people and telling them about God's love. He was tired and wanted to rest.

"Let's sail across the lake," said Jesus to his friends. So they all got into one of the fishing boats.

Jesus was very tired. He lay down in the boat with his head on a pillow. Soon he fell fast asleep.

Jesus' friends began to sail the boat across the lake. But suddenly a storm blew up. The winds began to blow. The sails on the little boat flapped. But Jesus was fast asleep.

The waves crashed and the boat rocked. Up and down, higher and higher. The water splashed and smashed into the little boat. It was going to sink! But Jesus was still fast asleep.

Jesus' friends were very frightened. They went to Jesus and shook him awake.

"Help! We're going to drown!" they shouted.

Jesus stood up.

"Be quiet!" he shouted to the wind. The wind stopped howling.

"Be still!" he shouted to the waves. The sea grew calm.

Jesus' friends didn't know what to say. First they were excited. Then they were afraid.

"He must be very special," they said to one another. "Even the wind and the waves do what he says!"

30
Jesus helps a little girl

One day a man named Jairus came to see Jesus. He was the ruler of the synagogue, and he was very important. Jairus needed Jesus' help.

Jairus was very sad. His little girl was ill. "I am sure Jesus will be able to help her," he said to himself.

Lots of people were trying to talk to Jesus. But Jairus pushed his way through the crowd and fell down at Jesus' feet.

"Please come to my house," he begged. "My little girl is only twelve years old, and she is dying. If you would just touch her, she would be well again."

So Jesus followed Jairus down the street. They had not gone very far, when some men arrived from Jairus' house.

"It's too late," they said to Jairus. "Don't bother Jesus. Your little girl is dead!"

"Don't be afraid," Jesus said to Jairus. "Just trust me. Your little girl will get better."

When they got to the house, there were lots of people outside, crying and wailing. They were making a terrible noise.

"There's no need to cry!" said Jesus. "The little girl isn't dead, she's just asleep!"

The people laughed. What did Jesus know?

Jesus went into the little girl's room. She was lying there, quite still. Jesus knelt down beside her and held her hand. Then he said, "Get up, little girl."

At once, the little girl opened her eyes and got up. She walked around the room. Everyone was amazed. She was not dead, she was alive. And she was hungry!

Jesus said, "Go and get her something to eat."

31

Jesus feeds a crowd

Jesus and his friends were tired. So one day they went into the countryside to rest. But a big crowd of people followed Jesus. They all wanted to be with him.

Even though he was tired, Jesus did not send the people away. So the crowd sat down on a grassy hill and listened to Jesus.

When evening came, Jesus knew that everyone was hungry. He asked his friend Philip, "Where can we buy food for these people?"

Philip was shocked. "But we are miles from anywhere! And it would cost far too much to buy food for everyone here!"

Just then, Jesus' friend Andrew brought a little boy to him. "This lad wants to give you his picnic," he said. "It won't do much good. He's only got five small barley rolls and two little fish."

Jesus smiled. "Tell everyone to sit down," he said.

Then Jesus took the picnic from the little boy. He picked up the barley rolls. He picked up the little fish. "Thank you, Father God," he said.

Jesus told his friends to share the bread and the fish with the people. He handed out the food to them, and they gave it to the people sitting on the grass. Everyone began to eat. There was enough for them all. There was so much food they could not finish it!

Jesus told his friends to pick up the food that was left over. The disciples went through the crowd. They filled up twelve big baskets.

Everyone was amazed. More than five thousand people had been fed that day! "Jesus must be a very special person," they said to one another.

32

The man who helped

Sometimes Jesus would answer a question by telling a story. One day, a man asked Jesus, "How can I please God and live with him forever?"

"Love God and love your neighbor," Jesus replied.

"But who is my neighbor?" asked the man.

So Jesus told this story:

"A man went on a journey down a long and lonely road. Suddenly some robbers jumped out from behind some rocks. They knocked the man to the ground and hit him and hurt him. They took his clothes and money, and then they ran away.

"Soon a holy man came down the road. He saw the man, but he pretended not to notice. He crossed over to the other side of the road.

"Then another man who knew all about God came down the road. He saw the man, but he pretended not to notice. He crossed over to the other side of the road.

"Finally a foreigner, a man from Samaria, came down the road. He saw the man lying on the ground, but he did not cross over to the other side of the road. No, he went to help him!

"The man from Samaria washed and bandaged the poor man's bumps and cuts. He gently helped him onto his donkey and took him to the nearest inn.

"'Please look after this man,' he said to the innkeeper. 'I will pay for everything he needs to get better.'"

Then Jesus turned to the man who had asked the question.

"Well?" Jesus asked. "Who was the good neighbor in that story?"

"The man from Samaria," replied the man thoughtfully. (He didn't really like Samaritans.) "Because he was kind."

"Be like him," said Jesus.

33
The good shepherd

One day Jesus told this story.

"Once there was a shepherd who had a hundred sheep. That was a lot of sheep, but he knew them all. Each one of them was special. Every day he counted them: 'One, two, three… ninety-eight, ninety-nine, one hundred.'

"One day the shepherd went to count his sheep: 'One, two, three… ninety-eight, ninety-nine…' That wasn't right. He counted again. But the hundredth sheep was still missing. It must be lost in the hills!

"The shepherd made sure that all the other sheep were safe. Then he took his shepherd's stick and walked over the hills, looking for the sheep that was lost. He looked in the brambles, he

looked on rocky ledges, and he looked down holes on the hillside. He looked high and he looked low. The shepherd looked everywhere. He did not give up.

"At last the shepherd saw the lost sheep. He hurried to rescue it. He was very happy that he had found it. The shepherd picked up the little sheep and put it on his shoulders. Carefully he carried it all the way home.

"'Look, everyone!' the shepherd said to his friends. 'Let's have a party because I've found my lost sheep.'

"All his friends were happy! The good shepherd had found his lost sheep."

Jesus looked at the people who were listening to him.

"This is a story about God," he said. "God is like that shepherd. Some of you are like that little lost sheep. God has come to rescue you, and when you start living to please him, God is as happy as the shepherd who found his lost sheep."

34
"I can see!"

"Help a poor blind man. Can you spare some money?" said Bartimaeus, a man who could not see. Each day he sat by the side of the road and held out his begging bowl as the people walked by.

One day Bartimaeus heard lots of footsteps. He heard voices and chattering and laughing. A crowd of people was coming along the road. What was happening?

"Jesus is coming!" said someone.

Bartimaeus had heard all about Jesus. Jesus talked to people about God. Jesus was a man who could do miracles. Bartimaeus wanted to meet Jesus. He shouted as loudly as he could, "Jesus! Help me!"

"Be quiet!" someone shouted.

"Jesus!" shouted Bartimaeus again.

"Stop shouting!" said someone else.

But Bartimaeus kept on shouting. He shouted so much he didn't hear Jesus call to him.

"Tell him to come here," said Jesus.

"Jesus is asking for you," said a kind voice.

Bartimaeus threw off his cloak and leaped to his feet. He put out his arms and felt his way through the crowd.

"What do you want me to do for you?" asked Jesus.

"I want to see!" said Bartimaeus.

"You will see!" said Jesus. "You believe that I can make you well, and so I will. Open your eyes."

Suddenly Bartimaeus could see the sunlight. He could see the blue sky. He could see the crowd of people. He could see Jesus. He had been healed!

"I can see!" Bartimaeus shouted again and again.

Then, shouting and leaping for joy, Bartimaeus followed Jesus down the road.

35

The man who climbed a tree

Zacchaeus was a little man who wanted people to look up to him because of his important job. Zacchaeus was the chief tax collector in Jericho. He was a very rich man. And he was a very rich man because sometimes he kept some of the tax money for himself! No one liked him. They called him a cheater.

One day Jesus went to Jericho. Everyone wanted to see him. The crowd pushed and shoved to get close to Jesus. They stood on tip-toe. They jumped up and down so that they could see. But Zacchaeus could not see anything. He was only a little man and could not see over the crowd.

Then Zacchaeus had a brilliant idea. He would climb up a tree so he could see. The little man scrambled up a nearby tree and sat on a branch. Now he was high above the crowd, and he could see everything!

Jesus walked slowly along the road, talking to the people around him. But when he reached the tree, he stopped.

Zacchaeus peeped out through the leaves. He wondered what would happen next.

He got a surprise.

Jesus looked up at Zacchaeus and said, "Come down here! I want to come to your house!"

Zacchaeus scrambled down. No one talked to Zacchaeus. No one ever wanted to go to his house. But Jesus did!

The two men talked and talked. Soon Zacchaeus knew he didn't want to be a cheater any more.

"I'm sorry I've been a cheater. I will give back the money I have taken," he said, "and more as well!"

Jesus smiled. From the moment he met Jesus, Zacchaeus was never the same again.

36

"Here comes the king!"

Jesus and his friends were going to the big city of Jerusalem. When they got near the city, Jesus sent two of his friends to get a donkey from the next village.

The two friends brought the little donkey to him. They put their cloaks on its back, and Jesus climbed on. He was going to ride into the city.

There were crowds of people standing by the road into Jerusalem. They knew all about Jesus, and they had come to meet him. Everyone was very excited. When they saw Jesus coming, some of them spread their coats on the road and made a path for the donkey to walk on.

Other people climbed up the trees. They cut down huge palm branches and put them on the road.

As Jesus rode by, they shouted for joy:

"King Jesus!

"Glory to God who saves us!

"Here comes God's promised king!"

The noisy crowd could be heard inside the city walls, and other people in Jerusalem wondered what was happening.

"What's all the fuss about?" they asked.

"Jesus is coming, the king on a donkey!" the excited people replied.

And so Jesus arrived in Jerusalem.

37

A very sad day

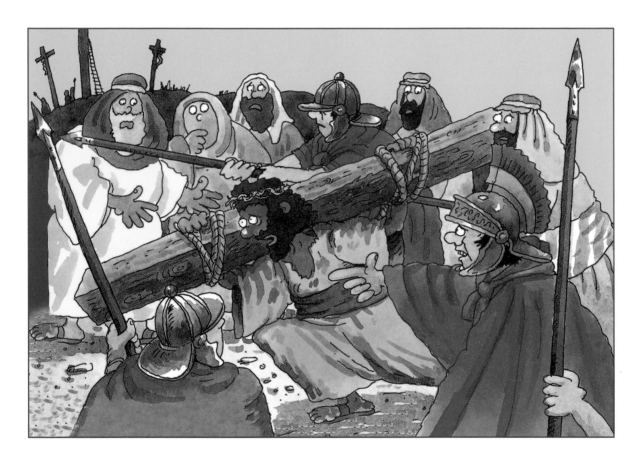

Jesus had many friends, but he had enemies, too. Some people didn't like what he said about God. Some people didn't like it when he healed people. Some people wanted to stop all the crowds of people following him. "Surely he can't be the Son of God," they said.

When Jesus came to Jerusalem, his enemies thought of a way to get him into trouble. They told lies about him and had him arrested. For a whole night, they asked him questions. Jesus' enemies did not believe he was God's promised king, and they wanted to kill him.

Then Jesus was taken to the Roman ruler of Jerusalem. He did not think Jesus had done anything wrong, but he was afraid of Jesus' enemies. So the Roman ruler said that Jesus must die.

The Roman soldiers took Jesus and dressed him up like a king. They made him a crown from thorny twigs. It hurt Jesus when the soldiers put it on his head. Then the soldiers made fun of Jesus. "Your majesty!" they laughed.

They made Jesus walk to a hill outside the city. All the way, people shouted cruel things at him. Then the soldiers nailed Jesus to a wooden cross.

Jesus' mother, Mary, and his friends watched and waited. They were very, very sad.

Jesus did not hate his enemies. "Father, forgive them," he said.

The sky grew dark, and after some time the earth suddenly shook. Jesus cried out in a loud voice, "Father God, I give you my life!"

And then he died.

"This Jesus really was God's Son," said a Roman soldier who had watched Jesus die.

Later that day, his friends took the body of Jesus and put it in a special grave – a tomb – in a garden. They rolled a very big stone across the entrance. Then, feeling very, very sad, they went home.

38

A very happy day

Early on Sunday morning, the third day after Jesus had had died, one of Jesus' friends came to the tomb. Her name was Mary Magdalene. She was very sad.

When Mary got there, she saw that the huge stone had been rolled away from the entrance. Who had moved it? She looked inside the tomb. It was empty! Jesus was not there.

Mary began to cry. What had happened to Jesus? Someone must have stolen his body! She looked inside the tomb again.

Then she saw two angels.

"Why are you crying?" they asked.

"Because someone has taken Jesus away," she sobbed.

"Why are you crying?" asked a voice.

Mary turned around. A man was standing behind her. She thought it was the gardener. "Someone has taken Jesus away. I don't know where to find him," she cried. "If you have taken him, please tell me. I will go and get him."

"Mary!" said the man.

Mary heard the voice. She knew who it was! It wasn't the gardener. It was Jesus! He was alive!

"Go and tell my friends that I am alive," said Jesus.

Mary knew that the disciples were in hiding together. They were sad and scared. This news would make them happy.

Full of joy, Mary ran to tell Jesus' friends, "He is alive! I have seen him with my own eyes!"

39
Thomas believes

Jesus was alive! Most of Jesus' special friends had seen him. He had come to the house where they had been hiding.

"Don't be afraid," Jesus had said. "It's really me!"

So the disciples knew that Jesus really had risen from the dead. They had seen the marks that the nails had made in his hands and his feet. Now they knew that he was alive. They were all very, very happy.

All except Thomas. He had not been in the house with his friends. He had not seen Jesus, and he just could not believe what the others

said. How could Jesus be alive again?

"But we've seen him!" one friend told him.

"He was standing here," said another.

"They must be dreaming," thought Thomas.

"Unless I see and touch the nail marks for myself, I will not believe it!" said Thomas firmly.

A week later, all the friends were together in their house. They had locked the door. This time Thomas was with them.

Suddenly Jesus was there with them. He greeted everyone, and then he turned to Thomas. Jesus knew what Thomas had been thinking.

Jesus held out his hands.

"Come on, Thomas," he said. "Touch my hands. Feel for yourself the place where the nails had been. I am alive!"

Thomas didn't need to touch Jesus. He knew that this really was Jesus. He was alive!

Thomas got down on his knees.

"My Lord and my God!" he said.

40

A picnic breakfast

After Jesus rose from the dead, his friends saw him many times. But they never knew when or where they would see him.

One evening Peter and some of his friends sailed out on Lake Galilee to fish. They threw their nets over the side of the boat. Then they waited. And waited. They waited all night, but they did not catch a single fish.

The fishermen were fed up. The sun was rising. It was time to go home for breakfast. As they sailed back home, they saw a man on the shore.

"Have you caught anything?" he shouted.

"No!" they replied.

"Throw your net over the other side of the boat," said the man. "Then you will catch some fish."

The friends were too tired to argue. They did as the man said. Suddenly the net was bursting with fish!

It was a miracle!

Then Peter knew. He looked at the man on the shore. "It's Jesus!" he cried. Peter jumped into the water and started to swim to the shore. He could not wait to be with Jesus again.

Jesus was cooking some fish over a fire on the beach. He had some bread, too.

"Bring some of the fish you've just caught," said Jesus.

The others brought the boat and the huge catch of fish to shore.

"Come on," said Jesus. "Let's have breakfast together."

So the friends sat down beside the fire to eat a meal of fish and bread. It was like having a picnic.

While everyone was eating, Jesus talked to Peter. He had a special job for Peter to do.

"I want you to teach other people about me," said Jesus. "Take care of them and be their leader."

41

Jesus is taken back to heaven

Jesus met with his friends many times. They walked together and talked together and ate meals together. He really was alive.

Jesus told them that he had to go away. They would not be able to see him, but he promised he would always be with them in a special way.

"I want you to tell the whole world about me, and I want you to teach people how to follow me," he said.

"But first you must wait in Jerusalem, and God will send his helper, the Holy Spirit, to be with you."

One day Jesus and his disciples were on a hillside near Jerusalem. They did not know that this was the last time they would see him.

"You will receive power when the Holy Spirit comes," said Jesus. "Then everyone in the whole world will hear about me."

Suddenly a cloud came down and hid Jesus from the disciples.

They looked around and up into the sky, but they couldn't see Jesus anymore.

While Jesus' friends were standing there, two angels came and stood beside them.

"What are you looking for?" asked the angels. "Jesus has been taken back to heaven. But one day he will come to earth again."

The friends remembered what Jesus had said. So they went to Jerusalem and waited for God to send them his helper, the Holy Spirit.

42
Good news for everyone

It was the day of Pentecost – a special harvest festival – and Jerusalem was very busy. People had come from all over the world to celebrate.

Jesus' friends were in Jerusalem, too. They were a little afraid now that Jesus had gone. But they were waiting for his helper, the Holy Spirit. Suddenly they heard a sound like rushing wind. It blew through the house. Then they saw what looked like flames, but there was no fire.

All of a sudden, the disciples didn't feel afraid any more. They left the house and went out into the city to tell people all about Jesus. They started to speak, and the visitors to Jerusalem were amazed.

"We can understand what they are saying!" they said. "How can they speak so many different languages?"

So Peter stood up and said, "God has done something wonderful today. He has given us his Holy Spirit, a sign that God is with us."

Then Peter told them all about Jesus. "God sent him to rescue us all, and you put him to death on a cross. But I have good news – he is alive! We have seen him.

"Say sorry to God for the wrong things you have done. He will forgive you," said Peter. "You can be a friend of Jesus, too."

On that day, three thousand people became friends of Jesus! They shared the things they had with each other, and they met together to pray and to praise God. Many people were healed in the name of Jesus.

Soon the good news of Jesus spread out from Jerusalem to other countries. The news has been spreading ever since, and now there are friends of Jesus all over the world.

Here's where the stories can be found in the Bible:

1 God makes the world, *Genesis 1:1-31*

2 The garden of Eden, *Genesis 2:15 – 3:24*

3 Noah's big boat, *Genesis 6:1 – 7:5*

4 The flood and a rainbow, *Genesis 7:6 – 9:17*

5 Abraham trusts God, *Genesis 12:1-5*

6 God keeps his promise, *Genesis 15:1-6; 21:1-5*

7 Jacob the trickster, *Genesis 25:21-28; 27:1-27a*

8 Joseph's beautiful coat, *Genesis 37:1-24*

9 Joseph goes to Egypt, *Genesis 37:25-36*

10 The princess and the baby, *Exodus 1:8 – 2:10*

11 "Let God's people go!" *Exodus 3:7 – 10:24*

12 Escape from Egypt, *Exodus 10:27 – 14:31*

13 The walls fall down, *Joshua 6:1-20*

14 A voice in the night, *1 Samuel 3:1-21*

15 Samuel chooses a king, *1 Samuel 16:1-13*

16 David and Goliath, *1 Samuel 17:1-51*

17 God takes care of Elijah, *1 Kings 17*

18 God sends fire, *1 Kings 18:16-46*

19 The girl who helped, *2 Kings 5:1-15*

20 Daniel and the lions, *Daniel 6:1-28*

21 Jonah and the big fish, *Jonah 1 — 3*

22 The baby in the manger, *Luke 1:26-38; 2:1-7*

23 Angels bring good news, *Luke 2:8-20*

24 Following a star, *Matthew 2:1-12*

25 Jesus and the fishermen, *Matthew 4:18-22*

26 Another special friend, *Mark 2:13-17*

27 Down through the roof, *Luke 5:17-26*

28 The two houses, *Luke 6:46-49*

29 A storm on the lake, *Luke 8:22-25*

30 Jesus helps a little girl, *Luke 8:40-42, 49-56*

31 Jesus feeds a crowd, *Luke 9:10-17*

32 The man who helped, *Luke 10:25-37*

33 The good shepherd, *Luke 15:3-7*

34 "I can see!", *Mark 10:46-52*

35 The man who climbed a tree, *Luke 19:1-10*

36 "Here comes the king!", *Mark 11:1-11*

37 A very sad day, *Luke 22:63 – 23:56*

38 A very happy day, *John 20:1-18*

39 Thomas believes, *John 20:19-29*

40 A picnic breakfast, *John 20:30 – 21:17*

41 Jesus is taken back to heaven,
   Matthew 28:18-20; Acts 1:4-11

42 Good news for everyone, *Acts 2:1-47*